BLACK HOLES IN SPACE!
THE WHAT'S AND WHY'S OF BLACK HOLES

Space for Kids
Children's Astronomy & Space Books

All Rights reserved. No part of this book may be reproduced or used in any way or form or by any means whether electronic or mechanical, this means that you cannot record or photocopy any material ideas or tips that are provided in this book.

Copyright 2016

There are lots of strange things in outer space. One of these things are black holes.

WHAT IS BLACK HOLE?

A black hole is a collection of massive objects that are strongly attracted to each other through gravity.

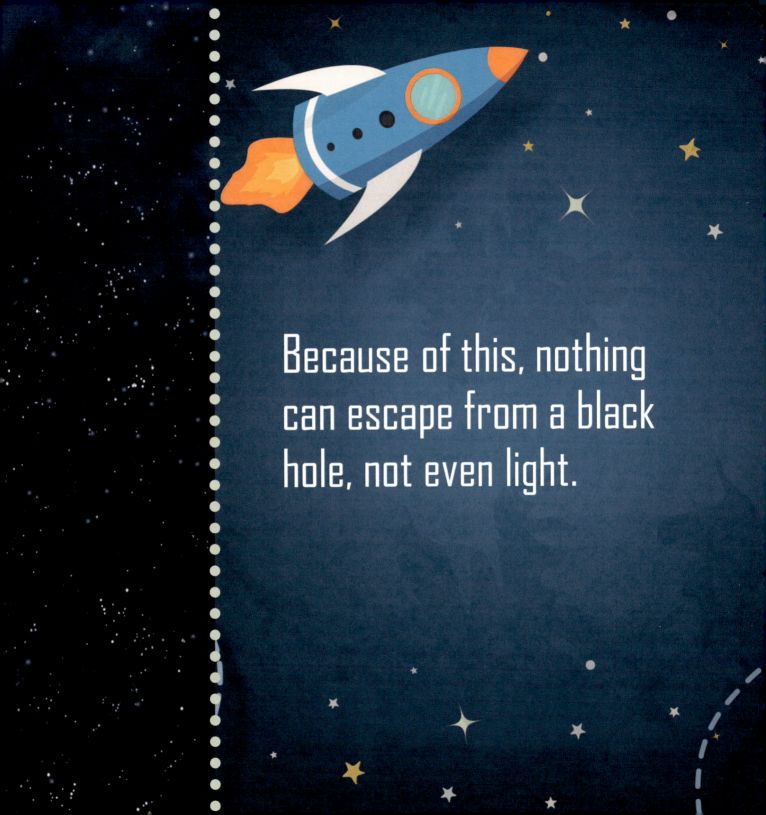

Because of this, nothing can escape from a black hole, not even light.

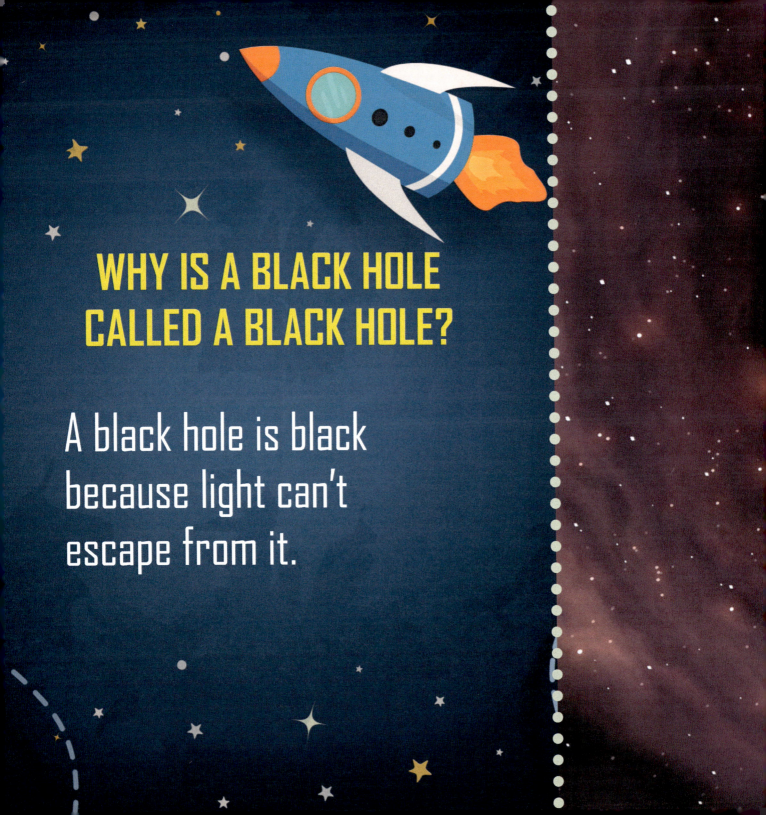

WHY IS A BLACK HOLE CALLED A BLACK HOLE?

A black hole is black because light can't escape from it.

Black holes come in different sizes. According to National Aeronautics and Space Administration (NASA), there are at least three types of black holes.

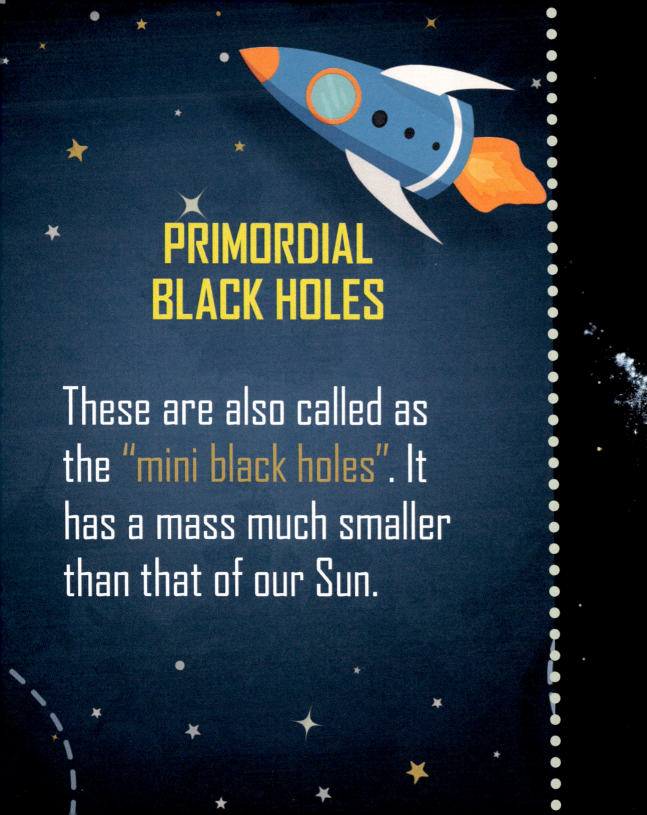

PRIMORDIAL BLACK HOLES

These are also called as the "mini black holes". It has a mass much smaller than that of our Sun.

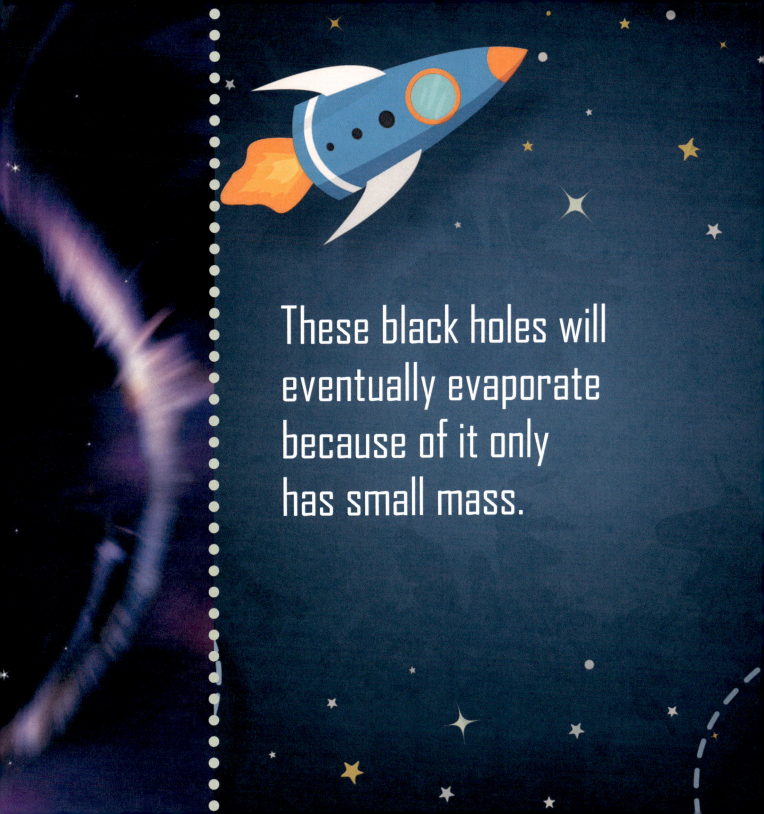

These black holes will eventually evaporate because of it only has small mass.

Mini black holes remains a theory since there's no observational evidence for miniature black holes yet.

STELLAR BLACK HOLES

These black holes are the most common. They are said to be approximately 20 times larger than the sun.

GARGANTUAN BLACK HOLES

These are massive black holes that are a million times larger than the sun. Can you imagine how big they are?

Did you know that Albert Einstein only expanded the theories about black holes in 1900's and the first idea of a black hole was introduced in 18th century?

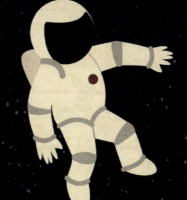

LET US LEARN SOME INTERESTING FACTS ABOUT BLACK HOLES.

- Cygnus X-1 was the first object considered to be a black hole. It was found in 1964.

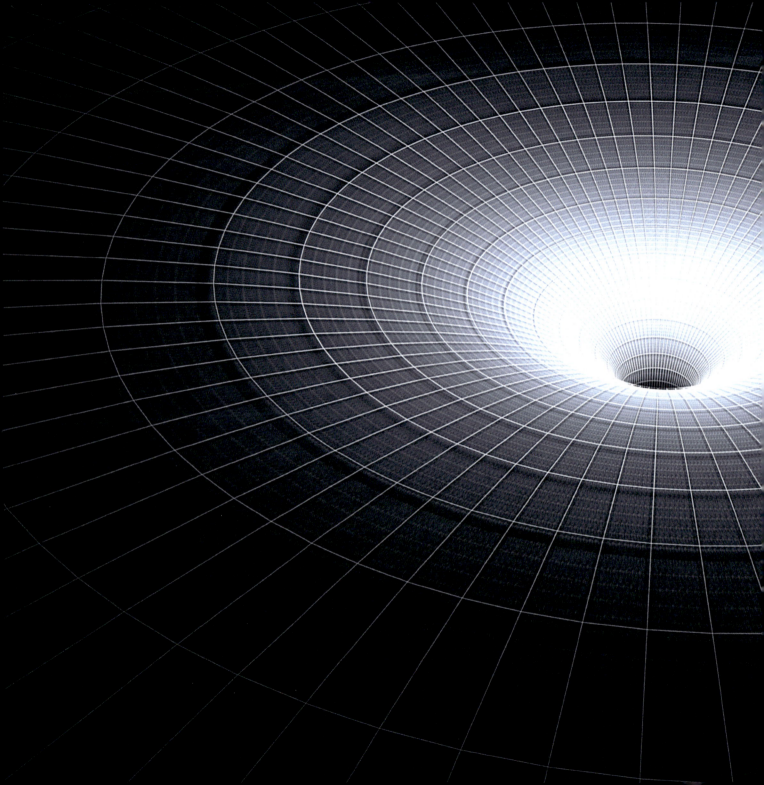

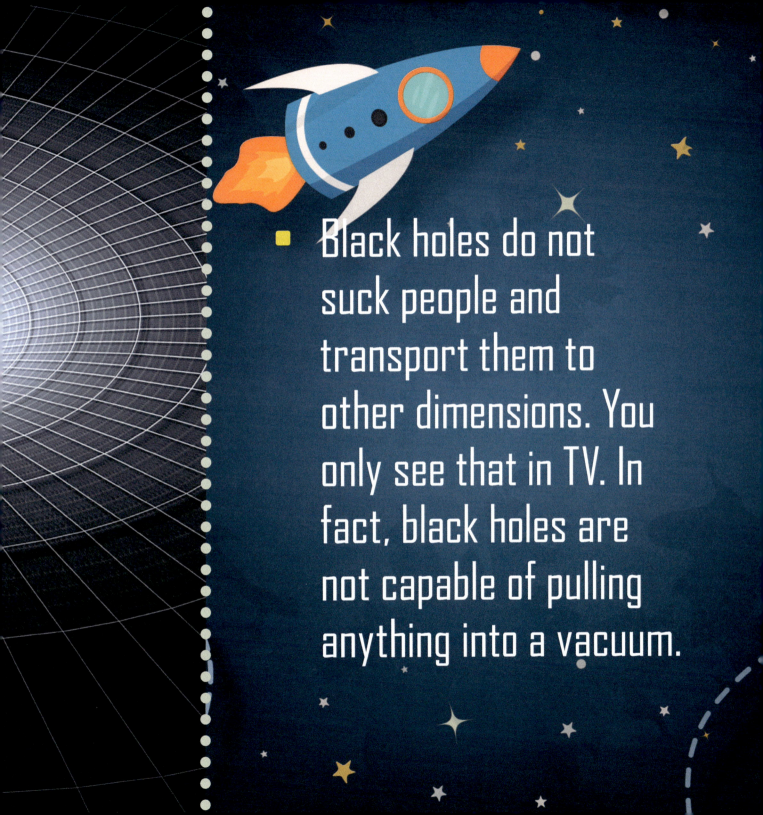

Black holes do not suck people and transport them to other dimensions. You only see that in TV. In fact, black holes are not capable of pulling anything into a vacuum.

- When a star or any object passes too close to a black hole, it can be torn apart.

- Galaxies, including the Milky Way, have Gargantuan black holes.

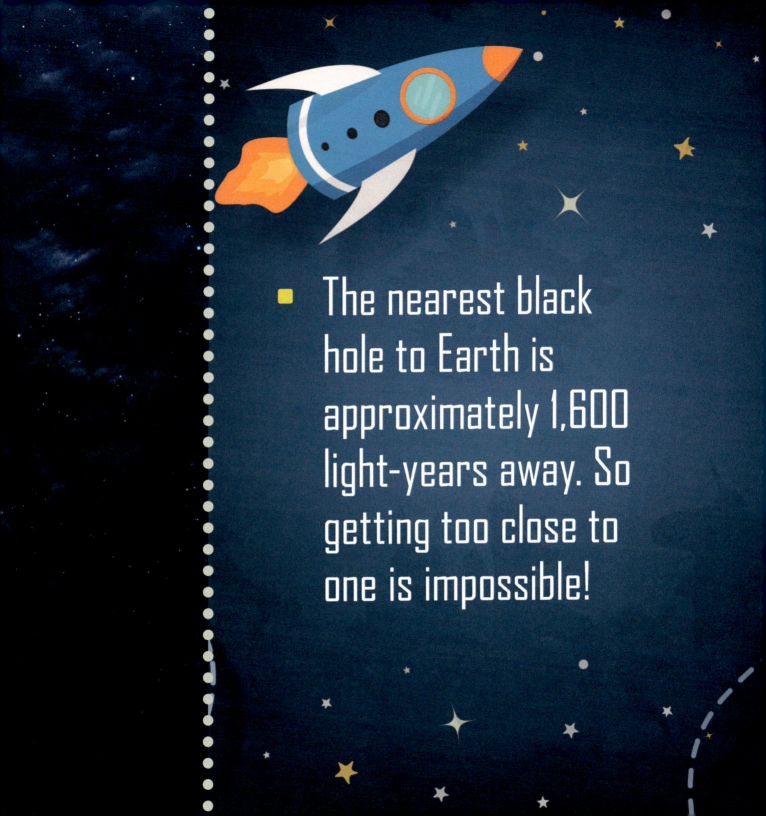

- The nearest black hole to Earth is approximately 1,600 light-years away. So getting too close to one is impossible!

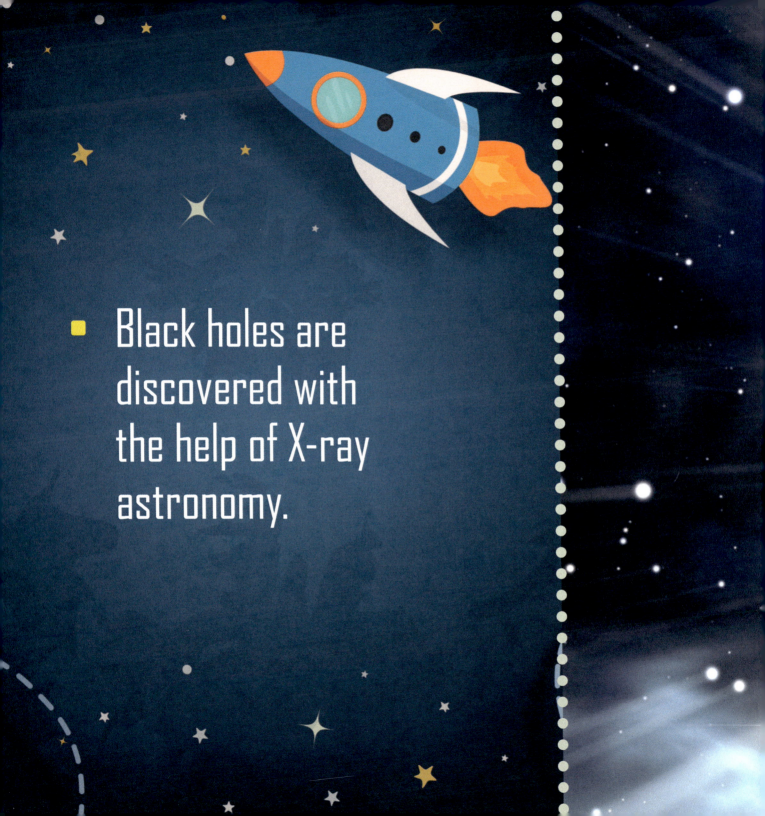

- Black holes are discovered with the help of X-ray astronomy.

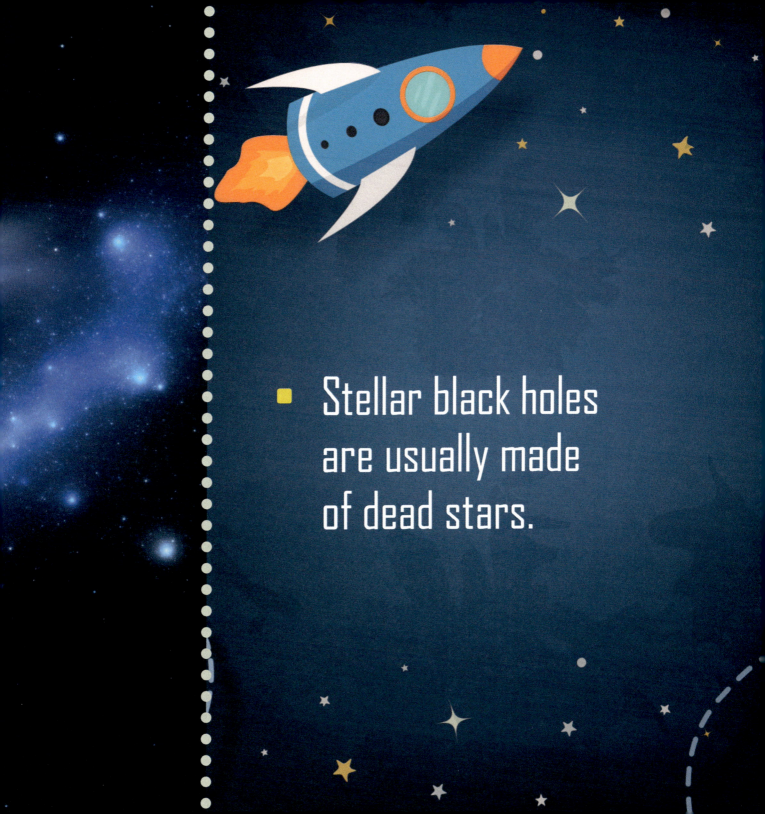

- Stellar black holes are usually made of dead stars.

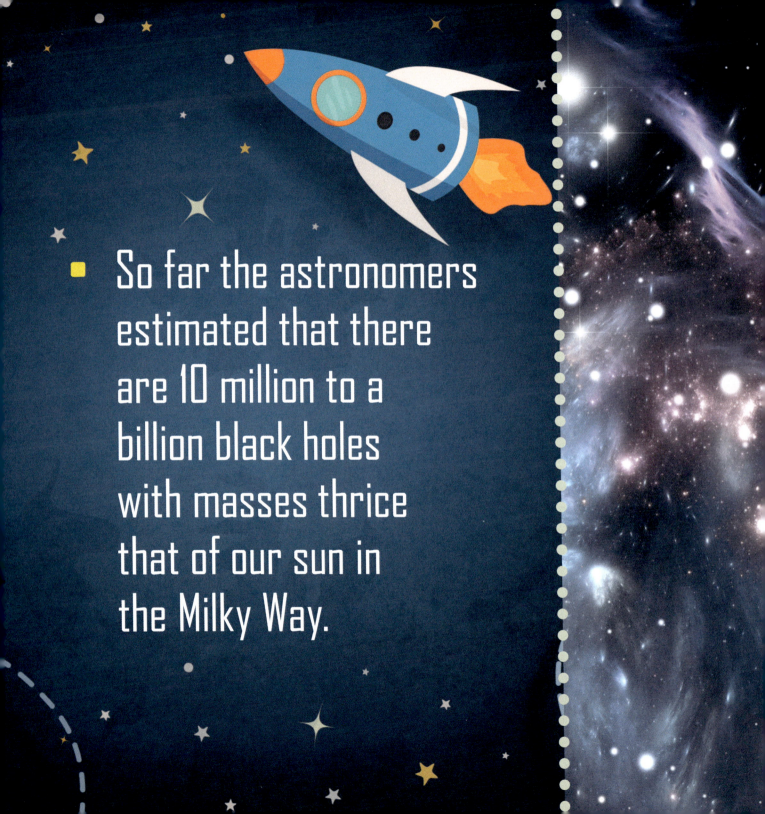

- So far the astronomers estimated that there are 10 million to a billion black holes with masses thrice that of our sun in the Milky Way.

Did you enjoy the things you learned about black holes?

Made in the USA
Coppell, TX
24 November 2021